The Summer of Shadow
by
Pat Payne

Order this book online at www.trafford.com
or email orders@trafford.com

Most Trafford titles are also available at major online book retailers.

Printed in the United States of America.

ISBN: 978-1-4269-4958-6 (sc)
      978-1-4907-0869-0 (e)

Library of Congress Control Number: 2010918033

Trafford rev. 09/18/2013

 www.trafford.com

North America & international
toll-free: 1 888 232 4444 (USA & Canada)
fax: 812 355 4082

FOREWORD

This true story is dedicated to the common Crow in the hope that those who read it will gain an increased understanding of this wonderful and remarkable corvine creature.

My original intent had been but to keep a log or diary of the experience as we nurtured this young bird back to health. However as days turned to weeks – then months filled with obstacles and triumphs, realized that we had all embarked upon the same journey and it was beginning to become a story.

And what good is a story unless it is told?

Enjoy, and thank you.

ACKNOWLEDGEMENTS

With many thanks to my wife Dot and son Scott who along with dog Murphy helped bring this experience to successful fulfillment. Up before dawn for almost three months of tending Shadow's needs while at the same time attempting to imprint him as little as possible. Well, OK, maybe upon occasion we did spoil him just a bit.

And to Gus. That bird of yesteryear when I was but sixteen. My very first Crow who taught me about his kind; yet nary a word written of him. Thanks for your hand, Gus in our successful endeavor to return one of your own to the wild albeit many moons later. This one's for you.

For that brief summer romance of a time when our expanded family circle came to include man, woman, beast and bird all interacting with one another for our mutual enjoyment, spiritual growth and enhancement.

THE SUMMER OF SHADOW

Where did it come from? A black satin lady's glove tossed with fingers splayed onto the brown leaves of the forest floor? That is what I felt the corner of my eye had caught and still recall my first thought as to how did that get there? A lady's glove?

Now bright shiny deep purple it turned. As I curiously moved closer the glove shifted shape and became a young fledgling crow peering up at me and seemingly just as confused as I was. I hesitated to gain my wits as to how I might best capture this forlorn looking creature while both our instincts took over and he accepted my slow but deliberate move to pick him up for a closer look. I think we both stared in wonderment, I know that I did.

And thus began our adventure with Shadow. The crow.

While he still had a few yellow pinfeathers he was pretty well along and aside from lacking any semblance of a tail appeared to have the necessary gear for attempted or limited flight. So as I carried him up the hill out of the woods towards our house I loosely and gently cupped one hand over him which he didn't seem to mind. Actually in retrospect he seemed exhausted from his earlier experiences out of the nest and quite content to go along for the ride. In the house we went to take a closer look at this young bird.

Wife Dot was the one who'd alerted me to the fact that she and dog Murphy had seen what appeared to be one of our young hawks on the ground and in distress. I had just returned home and they were both peering into the woods looking for further movement but all was still and quiet. After changing clothes I came back out of the house to search for whatever she had seen while she went back inside to resume getting ready for church.

I entered the house and when she responded to my call with a "What is it?" I replied I think we have our crow. Dot and I grew up as kids together and as a boy I'd had a crow named Gus. Over the years she often said she wished we could have one now where we lived as it is ideally suited for such a bird, on an Ozark hardwood ridge with few neighbors and a natural habitat for wildlife. We were both excited with our new boarder and quickly made a temporary shelter for him in a plastic laundry basket with lots of open slots for daylight and air. One of my favorite photos of Shadow was on his first day in "captivity." So tired he'd fallen sound asleep in my hand with his head hanging down and resting on our kitchen counter.

I said "captivity" because it was never our intention to keep him for a pet. Our mission was to nurse him to adulthood so that he could be turned loose and fly free. So from the first few days in the laundry basket he graduated to a wire critter type cage. It afforded more room for him to hop up on a natural tree limb roost we'd fashioned as well as a better look around his world that had obviously changed.

He took to it well and was never cowed or frightened by our activities. After a few weeks of being moved outside at first light and inside at dusk it became apparent that he was again in need of larger quarters. Son Tim to the rescue with a cage I'd built for his son's Iguana. Ample room for a fine young bird to begin some pre-flight training. During the day we rolled the cage from inside our front room foyer to the outside on the patio or sometimes the deck depending upon the sunlight and available shade and breezes. We kept him inside at night to avoid any marauding raccoon or coyote.

From day one we always had Shadow outside of the house and out of whichever cage might have been in use. He'd sit on have been in use. He'd sit on our hand or shoulder and Murphy the dog allowed him free run of what had been once his domain alone, our front patio and driveway. Good sort that Murphy as with curiosity he would accompany Shadow on his determined but oft clumsy walks up the black top curbing towards more interesting grassland and pine bark territory. Murphy and his bird – or – Shadow and his dog.

Those days Shadow walked wherever he went, wings being used only for maintaining balance, his short stubby beginning of a tail of little use. His first attempts at flight would be to gain access to the top of the planters boxes which were about four timbers high, or maybe a little over a foot. The fact that it seemed higher to him than that was obvious as his efforts were less than graceful. But by golly, he would get there clawing and flapping frantically. Only then once having achieved his climb/flight to the top seemed in a hurry to jump down and get on to explore something else. Always curious and always entertaining to observe was this young bird finding his way in the world.

The morning feeding rituals were always a fun occasion. While the first few days he had gulped down the raw hamburger in later weeks his preference leaned towards boiled chicken. Then one day he observed Dot in a front porch rocking chair eating her breakfast of Cheerios and his curiosity again took over. He hopped from her shoulder to the table to peer into her bowl and immediately helped himself to the little circles floating there. So then Cheerios in his water bowl became a daily treat, and it should also be noted that he became a great dunker. He loved to take whatever morsel of food he had in his beak to his water bowl and drop it in, sometimes to tear away a bit of the soggy bread or to deposit yet another bit of food into the bowl and stir them all around as if making a soup. Everything got dunked. The chicken, the bread, the Cheerios or then the Hi-Ho crackers or red grapes that had become yet another of his favorites. Even the crickets and worms would sometimes take that bath. Hence yet another nickname, Duncan in addition to Birdie.

The morning ritual had been between he and I, and he would get filled up after about

fifteen minutes and the rest of the morning until maybe 8:00 am would be devoted to gathering moss from between the bricks that formed the patio, or pecking fallen acorns, or gathering sticks or simply patrolling his patio in his parade like strut. Busy bird we would call him. Then when Dot came out he would get very excited flying up to her shoulder for more food as if he hadn't been fed for days. She became the bread lady and he clamored for the pieces she'd brought.

His first sustained flight and almost level instead of the usual downward paths was from my shoulder while sitting on our porch swing to the nearest cedar tree. About 20 feet before crashing into the snarl of limbs and coming to an awkward tangled stop, but landed nonetheless. After that first real flight experience he seemed to prefer walking over flying. Or I should say strutting in true crow fashion. Like the cock of the walk that he was.

And on such walks would be accompanied by Murphy alongside in a manner displaying the same curiosity as the crow. Our dog had never seen such a bird, or up so close as to be able to sniff him which Shadow accepted in a   very friendly way. Sometimes.

But oh those wonderful days when Shadow perched on my shoulder as I sat on the swing. He would cuddle close to my neck and just loved the swaying swinging motion of the swing as we chatted softly together.

A few days later  came his next serious attempt to fly. From my shoulder on the same front porch swing but this time in a different direction and a little further to a young hickory tree. But with the same resultant controlled crash. This one leaving him dangling upside down hanging by one leg as the limb he'd chosen wasn't stout enough to support him and was forced to droop ground-ward. Poor guy hung there upside down with wings flapping but not going anywhere because he wouldn't let go of what purchase he did have. So after plucking him from his latest undesirable perch we returned to the porch and placed him into the cage as the final daylight hours dwindled. This episode however left him with a sprained wing, drooping in an unnatural fashion below his still stubby tail not yet fully grown out.

He was obviously aware of his impairment because for days he attempted no further long distance flights. Just some flapping of wings as he climbed the rustic yard furniture to gain a higher vantage point where he would then perch to survey his present territory. He did successfully attempt short hop type flights to the backs of the rocking chairs or other porch furniture. One such piece of furniture located just in front of a window where he could look inside the house. He seemed to get bored if we left him alone too long and would perch there to wait for one of us to pass on our way to the kitchen that he'd

learned to associate with food. When he saw us would then begin a loud squawking to let us know "A bite of food would be appreciated here."

After a few days he appeared fit and ready to try again to solve that great mystery of flight that up until now had eluded him. We agreed that in the morning after wheeling the big cage from our foyer to the front porch we would see if he could be coaxed into flying.

Naturally after his breakfast he just roosted on my shoulder on the porch swing seemingly not at all interested in flying anywhere. OK, maybe a different launch pad would be in order. Maybe he was thinking "I've flown from this place before and those durn tree things always seem to get in the way." So we put him in what had become his favorite maple tree with two limbs at just the right height, a little over six feet off the ground. After much preening and a little chatter he flew from the tree to the roof of the house and then crow hopped to the roof ridge and then horror of horrors flew to the transformer of the electric pole that supplies the house. Naturally he liked it there and seemed amused at our attempts to attract him away. Finally he took wing and flew through the alleyway of trees that had been created by the utility crews to keep their lines clear and was out of sight in an instant. Sustained flight and

the furthest he'd been from "home" since we had taken him in.

Now the wait and wonder. Will he come back? But one thing for certain, he could really fly. And soon from the direction he had taken upon his departure we began to hear a muted caw separated by a few seconds before another timid caw. Almost like a "Here I am but I don't know where?" So up our road I walked slowly to see if I could locate this most recently soloed urchin. The trees were all fully leafed out and it was difficult to see any upper limbs or branches. To make it more difficult he seemed to be slightly on the move as his calls came from different directions, at first maybe 20 or 30 feet but occasionally like from a different area, and deeper into the woods towards the valley. To add to my anxiety the Coopers Hawks were on the hunt and their screeches echoed throughout that same valley Shadow seemed to be headed. I dreaded the thought of what a tasty morsel our young bird might be for them.

There I stood sometimes in the road sometimes in a neighbor's drive with a piece of chicken in my extended hand calling to Shadow in hope he'd want to come back for a morsel. But alas, all he would do was utter that sad little caw, and maybe even another, but always timid.

After hearing him change locations a number of times without ever catching sight of him I decided to leave him alone to work out whatever plan he would come up with. His calling continued but with longer intervals between the little pathetic caws as we sat on the front porch swing wondering how this would play out or if we would ever know how it did.

Finally around mid-day he showed up in a flight pattern that he was almost in control of. A little slip sliding to either side as he yawed generally in our direction over the road a little over tree top high. In fact too high and almost out of control. Like a little kid who while running downhill got to going too fast. So when he looked about to spiral down to our patio his altitude carried him instead into the taller trees over and behind the house. But he managed a landing instead of those earlier semi-controlled crashes we'd grown accustomed to. Finally a pretty respectable limb landing from where he immediately surveyed his new domain. He'd obviously been practicing.

He seemed comfortably settled in his new tree, a big oak now instead of his favorite smaller maple tree but as the afternoon wore into early evening he seemed a bit ill at ease. Calling that soft timid caw, maybe two caws, but always in a demure fashion. With a little over maybe an hour of light he worked his way onto a tree and a limb directly over our patio and I was pleased with the manner in which he secreted himself in the surrounding leaves. One of the first experiences of many to come that would show his natural instincts were in tune, and that we hadn't impaired them.

This was Monday June 29, Shadow's first day of total freedom. Three weeks from the day we took him in. We called it Shadow's Graduation Day. And a very long day it had been. I was drained.

I went to bed that night with thoughts of that darling little fledgling bird that once perched on the limb in his cage on the bay window shelf in the front bedroom. I could still see him in my mind gazing longingly at those trees just outside the window that must have seemed so huge and tall. And as I lay there our not so little guy anymore was roosting in one. I was so happy for him and began to reflect on memories of his many activities while growing to adulthood.

Shadow playing with his parakeet toy, sometimes worrying his reflection in the mirror or at times growling while attacking the little silver bell that hung below it. And then after mastering limited flight from ground up to the bird bath bowl, gathering sticks, hickory nuts, acorns or pine bark chips to soak therein. Or when he would merely perch to survey those treasures he'd deposited to soak, sometimes then cocking his head sideways and re-arranging those items. Those days at the patio table when while perched on a shoulder would feed and then begin tucking bits of food in your shirt pocket or beneath your shirt when he'd eaten enough and felt the urge to stash.

But click to the next morning when I was out front before daylight. As I had been every morning since this young bird had come into our lives. From the droppings on our brick patio could tell he'd stayed the roost. In fact as the day dawned could almost make him out in his cover of leaves. When Shadow commenced to move I called to him and he looked down saying good morning with a few gurgling caws. A gentle flap of wings accomplished his descent and soft landing onto the rooftop, whereupon a startled bug made a hasty but unsuccessful retreat. Crow hopping in pursuit, the quarry was dispatched quickly in a gulp.

Strutting back and forth on the gutter guards seemed to please him enough that he was reluctant to fly down. He would squawk, crouch and flutter his wings as young birds do when they beg for food, and then pace back and forth but couldn't bring himself to come to breakfast. That went on for twenty minutes before I went into the garage for a stepladder, and climbed up to him. I held out my arm and he hopped onto it, sitting there as I descended the ladder to the applause and thumbs up sign from neighbor Mike who'd developed a fondness for our wild visitor and had been watching the show. Shadow and I sat down together at the old food table whereupon he literally tore into the chicken and bread. Wife used to call it a patio table but many things in our life had changed since this bird's arrival.

As the day wore on he grew too pesky with Murphy and found himself in his favorite maple tree. We called it a time out although he didn't mind the location at all and of course it wasn't a punishment, simply relief for the poor dog. When Shadow got to be just too much, and he could really be an ornery and mischievous sort, we'd put him in his maple tree. What would be too much? One example is when Shadow picked up a twig and while holding it like a pointer in his beak strutted over to the unsuspecting Murphy and jabbed him rather soundly in the hind quarter. The dog leaped around spinning to his feet in a "What the?" while Shadow crouched and squawked his amusement at such great sport.

He could also get to be too much for Dot by persisting to pluck her earrings off the lobe of her ear. He learned to pluck a certain style cleanly but the ones that gave him trouble he would tug on rather aggressively and would have to be shooed away. To his time out tree.

While on that maple limb he loved to pull and tug at the stems of various leaves and after plucking them, bend over to drop and watch them fall. A trick that reminded me of my first crow that I had while I was a boy. His name was Gus, another story unto itself but one of his escapades used to include terrorizing the backyard neighbor lady by walking her clothesline, pulling clothes pins as he went just to watch her laundry fall to the ground. Thankfully she was also of very good nature.

While he would upon occasion fly to the ground near the birdbath or to various other yard locations he didn't appear to be interested in trying to gain the upper reaches of the surrounding trees. Just areas of the yard where he would go on exploratory walks, picking up morsels or simply objects of interest while on patrol.

One time such an object was a maple leaf that Shadow picked up by its stem and was strutting like a marching band member carrying a flag on a pole. Enter Murphy to rain on Shadow's parade by literally snatching that leaf from the bird's beak to dash across the driveway making his getaway. I never thought it was possible to see a look of surprise on a bird's face but I

assure you there it was, Shadow looking at me as if to say "Did you see that?" while Murph made sure I had seen his coup, trotting victoriously while shaking his grinning head side to side displaying his prize, the leaf. All right Murph! Score one for the dog!

But back to the second full day of freedom. As Tuesday drew to a close I placed Shadow on the limb of the Maple tree hoping that he would fly from there to the rooftop to pick out a roost tree. I was not disappointed as that is exactly what he did. Pretty cagey at that too as he didn't go straight to roost. He dawdled, perched on one of the gables in fading light that made me just a bit nervous because he was silhouetted and I remember thinking too late for the hawk, too early for the owl? But finally he dropped back to the shingles of the roof, strutted and hopped to the edge near the top and with a leap and a flap gained the limb he'd had his eye on. From there he seemed to survey the situation as he went limb by limb ever higher in the tree until I could no longer see him and the leaves were still. I remember thinking facetiously "My what a good parent am I."

The next morning didn't begin as nicely as the evening before had ended.

It had rained that night and he'd roosted in a tree behind the house so was not in sight when I came out the front. After searching the trees overhead and calling to him we heard him answer from the back but not with gusto. He seemed afraid and when we went out on the back deck there he was about 30 yards off in what appeared to be a soggy state

of confusion. He was not a happy camper from the night before and seemed scared. While he would answer feebly he wouldn't budge from his spot on that limb. After shuffling closer to the trunk, slowly and inch by inch he stopped. Stopped responding or moving, just stopped.

So we stopped too. We took on his demeanor and thought we can sit still and be quiet too if that's how you want it. When he did finally decide to move it was by short flight to another tree and to another limb at the same height and his body language suggested that's it. I'm staying right here. Son Scott had been with us that morning and now he and Dot went back into the house following our unsuccessful efforts to talk him in. I remained but when Shadow heard Dot and Scott exit the front of the house to get in Scott's car Shadow flew from his tree over the house towards them. He had developed an obsession with Scott whenever he left for work or returned and today was no different in spite of his earlier strange behavior. I went to the front where Shadow had landed in a tree over Scott's car and was finally able to coax him in for some breakfast of chicken and bread. It was then I saw that he'd had an encounter of some kind because he had suffered a scratch or blow to his head that left a slit of a bald spot maybe an eighth of an inch by a half inch. No blood or apparent real damage but no feathery hair that once grew there either. I was also uncomfortable with the way his right wing again drooped slightly instead of tucking up in a normal fashion. He'd definitely had an unfavorable experience of some kind.

After some eats and some healthy quaffs of water he began to take on the persona we'd grown accustomed to. Peck on his mirror and bell that had been removed from the big cage and now dangled from the front porch swing, strut around on the brick patio pulling up moss or anything else that needed to be uprooted and not to forget poor Murphy with a peck or two. Were it not for Murph's good nature and understanding Shadow would not have made it to adulthood.

That evening Shadow was not inclined to fly to the roof to seek a roost due to his drooping or re-sprained wing so we resurrected his intermediate cage and placed it on the ledge of the front bedroom bay window where he spent the night in safety. And my peace of mind. I didn't know what he'd run into out there but felt he wasn't ready to deal with it again so soon, whatever it was. The bird seemed satisfied as well with the night's accommodations, content to gaze outside from familiar surroundings. No complaints.

First light the next morning I checked to find him alert on his perch, looking out the window at the dawning and what this day might bring. He was a good boy always while in the house. To sleep early evening and while awake before dawn content to remain silent as he listened for sounds of his human's stirrings. But alert for sure, as I would see just the silhouette of his head turned looking in my direction from the hall letting me know he was ready. As I would carry his cage from the bay window bedroom to the front porch he would let out a token caw or two as if to say here I come world!

This day he limited his travels to the patio, perching on the backs of the rocking chairs with Murphy resting underneath between the rockers. That pair that I would sometimes refer to as dos amigos. While his drooping wing made him less inclined to fly it by no means cut down on his mischievous activities and the day was a good day for the cookie game. At least Shadow felt it to be a game, while I think Murphy felt it to be something not at all amusing let alone fun. So many human characteristics did that bird possess. No matter how much food would be available to Shadow, the loud crunch of Murph's jaws breaking that cookie (dog biscuit) into bits would attract Shadow like a duck to a June bug. The bird would come running to get real close, tilt his head so as to not miss anything and then instantly dart right under the dog's grinding jaws to snatch the biggest piece of biscuit in sight. Sometimes Murph would growl and snap at Shadow but Shadow would make his hasty retreat with a hop and a flap of wing every time. Once though Murphy did bump and roll Shadow squawking onto his back but I think more by accident than on purpose.

So as this day's adventures drew to a close I thought for his own protection, better to put him in his big cage for the evening. He was sitting on the back of the porch bench closer to the west woods and when he saw or heard me noisily rolling the big cage out from the garage took immediate wing into those woods. While it was strictly a level or straight line flight with no altitude gained, it was at least honest flight and to a tree about 10' off the ground. I didn't know if it was the noise or the sight of the cage but I was pretty certain it was indeed the cage that spooked him. He was asserting himself and let me know – no cage, no thanks. I like it out here.

Well he was out, it was late and soon to grow dark and the best thing I could do now was to leave him alone and observe. Limb by limb he gained some height in that tree and when reaching the level he wanted took wing again, this time heading into the woods behind neighbor Mike's house. Oh well, maybe good news bad news again in these adventures as that particular neck of the woods was frequented by the Great Horned owl. So while that thought was a bother I assured myself that it wasn't the time of year for their visits. Good night Shadow, watch your back, OK buddy? Live and grow big so that you can be the one to harass them as will be your nature.

The next day dawned and no Shadow. Until neighbor Mike came walking down our road with Shadow perched on his arm coming along for the ride. Mike was grinning from ear to ear, his family had been sharing the Shadow adventure but until now at our house or from a distance. Now, this morning while they were on their front porch in comes Shadow from their rooftop and swooping to a landing right in their midst. Shadow made the transfer from Mike's arm to mine and I walked him home for some breakfast that he was more than happy to gulp down. No stashing this morning.

We spent time with Shadow the rest of the day, Dot, Scott and I engaging in those fun activities of watching the bird scouting the patio for choice twigs or acorns to be deposited in the bird bath or his water bowl. Or Shadow exercising another of his favorite pastimes, flying to Scott's shoulder to pull his hair while then perching atop his head. And as evening drew near you could see Shadow looking skyward thinking "best be finding a good place to bed down pretty soon" whereupon he would fly to the roof and then strut the ridge to the east or maybe west while deciding which tree it was to be for this night's roost. And then to the tree. And then peck and pull a few leaves to re-arrange or drop. And then to another limb – and another – working his way higher until he would be out of sight.

These days before he hooked

up with the wild crows were spent roosting in the tall oaks that surrounded our house. He didn't seem to have a favorite or was perhaps exercising his survival skills by not being predictable. So in those early dawn hours when I would step outside with his breakfast could never know where he was going to be. Unless son Scott left for work at first light or sooner. When that happened Shadow would announce his presence and not wait for me, instead flying straight to Scott as he walked to his vehicle and light on his head or shoulder. The bird almost seemed obsessed with him.

Another interesting routine Shadow developed was helping Murphy guard the house. Yes, Murphy was the watchdog and Shadow took it upon himself to be the watchbird. When an unfamiliar car or person would pass our drive on their way up or down the hill Murphy would bark his annoyance and warning while running to the boundary imposed by the invisible fence. And Shadow would take immediate wing flying directly over the dog cawing just as loud and threatening as the dog was barking. When Murph hit his boundary and stopped in his tracks at the edge of our drive, Shadow did too, flaring up to catch an overhead limb while still scolding the intruder with his loud cawcawcawcaws. You just had to see and hear it to believe it. And I must tell you that by the look on one early morning jogger's face, she DIDN'T believe it.

Thursday August 19 the bird showed up later that morning than had been his habit, although his habit was becoming less predictable as he was showing up anywhere now from before 6:00 AM to as late as 10:00. He came right to the table on the front patio after no announcement that he was in the neighborhood. Although as soon as he lit on the table other crows were heard from behind the house. The crow clan had been patrolling our ridge more frequently as of late. As if they were aware of our "prisoner" and kept trying to get a closer look. It was during those flyovers when they would shout out their calling caws that Shadow would tilt his head skyward with an inquisitive look as if  to say to me "Did you hear that?" But aside from that he displayed no interest or inclination to join them.

These days of young adulthood were spent mostly in the area of our front yard and porch. When he tired of picking moss or gathering other treasure would perch on the backs of the rocking chairs, fire pit furniture, stone grinding wheel, porch swing or of course his favorite maple tree always on the same limb that he'd finally just about plucked bare of any remaining leaf. During these days when Dot and I would return home from our walk or errand, while driving down our driveway, there would be Shadow. Almost as if waiting for us because he would joyously announce our arrival as a validation of Murphy's tail wagging trot. Dot began to remark "He's never going to leave." But of course, he would. And he did.

SHADOW HOOKS UP

The day that Momma Bird collected her previously orphaned fledgling Shadow had been perched unusually high in an oak behind the house, high up enough to be visible over the rooftop from the front patio. And also high up enough to be more easily seen by the crow clan that had been rather active this day. Singles sailing over the house with an occasional pair of birds flying a parallel course with the valley to the east and not silently. They were making their presence known with loud caw – caws as they flew over. As stated earlier we felt they were aware of our "prisoner" and today seemed to be the day they intended to do something about it.

I was reminded of a war party of Sioux or Blackfeet as the five or six approached from the east valley, leapfrogging one another as they made their way to Shadow still on his perch. Rather slowly and tree by tree, more hopping than flying but steadily and quietly on their way. When two trees away, the Momma Bird took over leaving the others behind to wait. Closer she came branch by branch or sometimes two, but always closer while Shadow perched and peered off in a different direction, seemingly disinterested. It was a thing of beauty, this mother approaching her young one very cautiously but certainly coming in to hook up and as I watched was warmed immensely. It was truly a dance of love and beauty. When a few feet distant she stopped and began to preen her feathers and Shadow did likewise, both seemingly rather nonchalant, but she kept inching slowly closer all the while. Almost indifferent towards each other, but they were hooking up. And when the game was over Shadow leaped downward from the branch towards the north valley with Momma on his tail in hot pursuit as was her party she'd left a few trees back. All were gone in an instant amidst an excited flurry of Kaw-Kaw-Kawing joy echoing back out of the valley behind the house and Shadow's life had indeed taken wing. We saw him no more that day nor did he roost near the house that night. He was now a crow clansman. Shadow didn't live here anymore.

Oh the mixed emotions. Starting to feel like an empty nester while at the same time so happy and proud that it appeared as though we had accomplished our mission to nurse that once forlorn helpless fledgling into a real live wild bird. The joy of seeing that once tiny and injured bird now turned big guy crow handle his wings so beautifully as he flew where he wanted to go. No longer just an unattainable dream as when he gazed out his bedroom bay window into the upper reaches of those ever so huge trees he could only imagine. Hallelujah – Praise God.

Funny though because he returned the next morning an hour or so after first light and was happy to have his breakfast of chicken, bread and dog biscuit pieces. In fact he hung around all morning doing as he had always done before. Pestering his dog, checking his bird bath treasures but now having to duck his head as the bluebirds were very displeased with his presence. Their family was ready to fledge and their nesting box was smack dab alongside the bird bath so while they proceeded to dive bomb him he was content to just squawk his displeasure at them as they streaked ever so closely to his head. After tiring of the bluebird bombardment and being satisfied that his bird bath treasures were safe he took his leave with a swooshing low level flight away into the east woods.

The evening of the same day I really didn't expect him to show since he'd been here late that morning but all at once he lit in the upper reaches of his maple tree around 6:00 pm. absolutely unannounced as with the silence of a stealth aircraft. Murphy saw him first and as he stared into the treetop I got off the porch swing to walk out on the bricks for a closer look whereupon Shadow executed one of his beautiful effortless takeoffs by stepping off the limb and catching the air with his first wing stroke that carried him toward the roof but turning and spiraling down to the umbrella table and a graceful soft thump of a landing with a look towards me like "What's up?" I could almost feel him say "I'm in a bit of a hurry right now, my pals are waiting and I don't have much time to spare so I'll just grab a bite and run." And that he did but not before a trip to the birdbath to soak a chunk of bread; and then off over the house amidst a few welcoming caws and he was gone.

Shadow's next morning visit began with his caw – cawing from his treetop perch as I stepped onto the front porch. But today he'd brought a few of his clan and upon leaving his perch to fly down to the table another crow was flying from the east just over the rooftop to a nearby tree whereupon before lighting that one announced his presence with a load "Caw – Caw" which was one of the few times one of the natives was so bold and visible. At that same time I saw what I've come to call the "Momma Bird" arrive from the east to take up a point of vantage on one of the same limbs she'd first approached her orphaned boy a few weeks ago. Shadow fed on some chicken and beef but was mostly interested in old waffles and Hi Ho crackers. The two visiting adult birds remained quiet all along. When I could tell that the feeding visit was about over Shadow took a whole Hi Ho cracker in his beak and flew off the table towards the bath but this time when over the driveway executed a great low level almost 180 degree turn and grabbing some altitude and velocity flew over the roof towards that Momma Bird and was soon out of sight. All of them gone now along with "junior."

Tuesday August 24 I went to

the front patio a few minutes after 6:00 AM to greet a beautiful morning. No breeze but delightfully cool compared to the previously scorching days of 100 degrees. Coffee in hand along with Murphy I went to listen for whatever activity would be forthcoming. Murphy was as much a part of this daily routine as my morning coffee. He would take up an observation position looking and listening just as I did.

First verbal crow activity had started close to 7:00 AM from over a quarter mile away to the east, sounded like maybe three or four birds cawing their plans to the others to gather up. The first visual sighting at 7:20 AM upon Shadow's arrival without even a thump as he lit on the roof over the garage. Instead of coming to the table he'd decided to do a little housekeeping snatching a piece of bread left on the roof from yesterday. As he strutted with his bread piece the bird I'd come to call Momma lit in one of the tall oaks behind the house but in full view of me in the drive and talking to Shadow on the roof. She's a beautiful big radiant purple black adult and this day was bolder or less afraid as she'd been the previous days which pleased me greatly. I softly talked reassuringly to her that we would cause no harm and that she was certainly welcome. She turned and cocked her head as if to acknowledge while I returned to the patio table and Shadow whom while I was conversing with momma had been busying himself filling his gullet like a pelican, a good sign that he would be taking wing rather quickly with his provisions. And sure enough that is exactly what he did; taking morsels to momma as he flew with a whoosh over the roof and as he cleared the ridge his guardian left her limb in pursuit of her boy and breakfast.

But another treat was in store for us because after having been gone for only a few minutes Shadow reappeared on the roof, having lit on the backside and then walking over to the front to then fly down to the patio table. And as he lit, momma sailed right into the tree that we were under and gave a loud caw-caw to announce her arrival. The closest any of the native birds had ever ventured.

Now again Shadow fed and immediately began filling his gullet with bits of cookies (dog biscuits) and when his pelican beak was full flew to the west but less than thirty yards to a limb where he deposited a few treats for mom who then promptly joined him there. Shadow flew to the ground below the tree to begin stashing and while momma bird dropped to lower limbs was just a little reluctant to go to ground so near to me still at the table. After being able to delightfully observe their ritual for a few minutes it was over too soon and they both sailed off to the north.

I doubted we'd see them again that evening as the pattern seemed to have developed where we'd see them in the morning but not later that same day. I found myself to be more overjoyed with Shadow's acceptance into his clan than sad over our "loss" of that once darling little fledgling bird, thence turned mischievous comedian and now turned wild and free, flying those skies he'd once only wishfully gazed upon. Thanks Be to God, again.

Thursday August 26 was Shadow's second day of being a no-show, and it dawned beautifully cool, in the mid 50's and certainly a welcome relief from this month's heat wave. But no Shadow at first light or even until we decided to go for our walk around 8:30 am.

Upon our return drive home and just as we turned from Antire on to Little Antire Road I heard him call. Yes, I know, how could I be certain it was him? Well of course I could not prove it, but I was beginning to sense an ability to converse in the Crow language. And what I heard in that CawCawCaw (not hyphenated because they were rapid fire Caws) was Shadow shouting his "Hey" upon recognizing our returning vehicle and perhaps my arm and white sleeved T-shirt out the window.

When we pulled down the driveway it appeared as though he hadn't returned home, but when Dot stepped from the vehicle I saw her looking into the trees because there lit Shadow while calling to us like "Where ya been?" To use an expression, as the crow flies it's about one quarter mile from where Shadow had called to us on Antire Road and over a half mile by road. He could have easily beaten us to the house but I suspect and feel rather strongly that he had "shadowed" the vehicle as we made our way home.

And pardon my joy again because our   big boy bird began a loud
series of come on caws, the Caw-Caw-
Caw-Caw types as he called to his clan
that we could hear calling back from
down in the valley. He had become
a real live full fledged card carrying
member of his crow family as was
evident by the exchange of chattered
clamoring over the airwaves.

To add to his verbal's he leaped from
his treetop and executed a beautiful
full powered 360 degree flight

pattern, at altitude so his buddies might observe, landing where he had taken off from to call some more. Reminiscent to me of the early plains Sioux or Crow warrior riding his horse in circles signaling a message to his far off hunting party. I was indeed learning their language and the consensus appeared to be from his pals "Do what you must; we'll wait here for you." Whereupon Shadow again flew from his perch making another full circle only this time descending to a tree near his bird bath where he again voiced call. It appeared as though he hadn't come to feed, merely to visit but I walked towards him with a morsel in hand hoping to entice him to my arm. When I got close he quit calling and flew to my shoulder while commencing the baby talk we used to exchange when he was but a pup.

He was more interested in the Hi Ho cracker I had than the piece of chicken and after taking it flew to the pine chips on the ground to stash. I retreated to the front porch swing to give him some space and no sooner had I sat down that he glanced my direction before taking flight into the woods towards the east valley where his clan could be heard calling. I find it difficult to express my joy over his progress as it unfolds daily. He is definitely a big boy now.

Friday August 27, Shadow stopped by but almost as if to say goodbye. I'd come out at first light and aside from being a beautiful cool morning it was quiet. Around 6:20 AM the clan could be heard gathering in the valley to the east and then our boy could be heard cawing his way closer to the house. It grew quiet for about five minutes and then here he came winging his way from the west directly over the house about twenty feet high. Acting more the Comanche every day now, he had announced from the east but came in from the west. This bird's giving lessons now instead of only taking them. Straight into the east tree behind the house and in plain view he lit while announcing his arrival to all. His buddies replied but stayed where they were. As I talked to Shadow from the drive he began his leaf game, pulling oak leaves from their limb and watching them fall to the forest floor. Ever the clown no matter how mature becoming. I almost had the feeling that with his actions he was saying come on up and play with me awhile.

From that tree he swooped down over my head then back up into the bird bath tree to perch and call for just a bit before coming down to light on the driveway nearer to Murphy than me. Strutting his hello past his dog towards me I stooped to extend my hand that he hopped onto. I raised him, beak to beak we chuckle talked for a bit but as I headed for the patio table he bolted to a tree just west at the edge of the drive. I hesitated, thought well OK and walked to the front porch swing. No eats, maybe just a visit? A few loud caws from his latest perch and he was up –up and away northward over the rooftop and quickly out of sight. The clan could then be heard in that valley to the north and soon they were all gone. Shadow was not My Shadow anymore. Now he was being his own Crow and my empty sadness was exceeded only by my great joy to see him blossom so.

After that visit I reflected on the question, how can one feel so glad and sad at the same time? He'd become such a handsome bird. No, more like majestic. And now he was cutting the cord. Now learning his Crow lessons from ones more suited than I for that task. But I'm OK. Shadow is doing what he must do and I will attempt to take care of my end of that beautiful bargain he and I, total strangers at the time, struck that sunny June morning. That morning that I told him I will get you out of these woods and your temporary predicament, and all you need to do is grow, get strong and stretch those wings to join your brethren. And today oh my, you should have seen that big and wonderful bird fly!

Saturday August 28, Shadow was a no show. At least visibly, because his presence was made known by the clamoring of his clan in the east valley working their way towards our house. As they drew near one lone bird called from up our road and then after a few minutes again from the west side of the house and much closer. In fact from one of the oaks right alongside the house. I felt certain our guy was about to execute one of his graceful "Good Morning" swoops over the patio perhaps then to wheel left and up to the rooftop or right and down to the food table or better yet my shoulder. It didn't happen. Nothing happened. Total silence. The clan could not be heard nor did I hear the whooshing of Shadow's wings in departure. He'd executed one of his now patented stealth departures most likely down the hill behind the house and the valley below. Sunny – but no Shadow today.

Sunday dawned; I let Murphy out and then brewed the coffee. Pocketed some dog biscuits wondering if Shadow's name was on one and remember feeling a bit pitiful as I took his container of food out of the fridge before going outside. Sitting on the porch swing with Murph waiting for our paper man the clan at first light could be heard but distantly and beyond the east valley. The coffee went down rather well in the silence that followed. Paper man came down the drive, Murph went to greet him and fetch the paper that was carefully and deliberately dropped for his convenience. The delivery man smiled as he watched Murphy get a grip on the heavy edition and then trot in my direction with his tick-tocking tail wagging with pride as he did his job. I got my paper, Murph got his cookie and the paper man was back on his route. I poured another coffee, sat in the swing gently rocking and thanked God that dogs didn't fly.

Later that day, when asked how Shadow was doing these days I jokingly told neighbor Jody that he's doing just fine but I am suffering post-partum depression. She smiled and shared with me something that mothers have always known but that I hadn't fully appreciated. "Your child has grown up and now you must do the same." Yes. But oh those starkly empty cages sitting eerily in the garage, little cage atop the big cage and so totally quiet.

Four empty days passed and while we had seen no Shadow there were a few times when a member of the clan passed by with an occasional caw. Then one afternoon our human clan was gathered on the front patio when we heard two or three birds behind the house and off to the east. I went further out in the drive to investigate and in one of the oaks where the clan

had first claimed their own perched two fine birds. The one a bit more secretive by her positioning amongst the leaves I felt to be Momma Bird, still giving lessons to her wayward boy. As I was trying to convince myself the other was indeed our Shadow, that one dropped into his old familiar crouch and flutter and while looking straight at me executed that little dance and guttural squawking that I had come to love and now grown to so sadly miss. I felt it to be a heartwarming gesture by Shadow, telling us that all was well and he would be forever grateful for what we had been able to do for him. I think he said "Gotta go now, gotta take care of my end of that bargain we made back on that June morning, you and me." Shadow doesn't live here anymore, but he is home. Now fully re-claimed by his own Crow Clan.

EPILOGUE

Tuesday morning following the Labor Day Holiday dawned a bit overcast with a promise of rain. The date was September 7, 2010, exactly three months and one day from that Sunday morning Shadow had entered our lives. We had coffee on the front patio as has been our custom and the crow clan could be heard in their valley off to the east. Distant but not too far to aim my good ear in their direction to see if I could discern Shadow's voice. Maybe a stretch even for a good ear but you know what they say about hope, and in my heart it did still spring, though reserved.

They never did work their way closer and soon our activities, lacking Shadow's presence fell into our somewhat boring human norm. Son Scott took Mom on an errand while running a few of his own. I retired to my office to check e-mails. Stupid computer/printer rebellion type of day that fit right in because as of late I had finally come to admit that the bird's absence had me bummed. While I might boast of his finding his wings and claiming the sky and his clan as his own, I really felt he would have stopped by since that time last when he had along with Momma Bird to give me his familiar crouch and growl gurgle before taking his leave.

I had to admit that my feelings were hurt. And my ego, now feeling that maybe I didn't really know the crow as well I'd thought. I was puzzled as to why we hadn't seen him in over a week and began to fear for his well being.

The rain began in a half hearted drizzle and went in and out of that mode for maybe an hour when I heard caws calling from the back of the house. From the north valley and where my office window faces. I didn't make a move to go outside. Even though they were the familiar type calls, and I had even heard one that appeared closer. Sure it sounded like Shadow but by now felt I was only kidding myself and wasn't going to play the fool by dashing upstairs. When I finally made a move it was while listening to Dot open the back door and begin talking - to Shadow. I stepped outside and there he sat perched on an overhead oak limb so I went back in for a piece of bread to see if he would be enticed to fly to my arm. As I held the bread aloft for him to see, he flew to a limb more suitable for his final approach and after displaying his old familiar crouch flutter and growl, flew down to my outstretched arm.

Murphy had been whining excitedly while taking all this in and Shadow dutifully hopped down to greet his dog properly. Didn't even peck him, just strutted up to him for a friendly "Hey" and a Murph sniff before winging back up to the deck railing. So we all then held a joyous reunion on the back deck. Shadow acting his old self, pulling tufts of bread from the piece that Dot held while at times reverting back to his earlier habit of letting her respond to his begging by placing pieces in his open beak. Kill the fatted calf? No but we sure did come up with some fresh juicy bits of raw hamburger that Shadow wolfed down and then stock piled in his pelican beak, usually a sure sign of his impending departure. With gullet a bulging he flew to a nearby limb to stash and returned immediately for more. On that last return we had a nice chat, beak to beak, just me and him. He preened my mustache, cocked his head to look in my eye and gave my shiny tooth a peck when I laughed after his investigation of my nostrils. We both laughed and gurgled, I told him we loved him and he told me to quit being such a wuss. Then he took wing through the dense woods and like a shadow, swiftly, silently, gracefully disappeared towards the east valley. I'm better now, it is a beautiful rainy day and all is well on this Ozark hardwood ridge in crowdom.